COUNTRY COOKING

Consultant Editor:
Valerie Ferguson

HERMES
HOUSE

Contents

Introduction

The character of country cooking does not depend on geography. Whether you live in a city flat, a town house or a rural cottage, you can enjoy the pleasures of wholesome food, plainly cooked, but packed with flavour. The secret of country cooking is the use of the freshest, seasonal produce. There is something special about the first tender vegetables of the summer or the succulent berries of the autumn. Spring lamb is almost a cliché and what could be more sustaining on a cold winter's day than a rich pie brimming with chicken and leeks.

Few people these days have the time to grow vegetables and fruit or to catch wild trout, but modern transportation brings produce to even inner-city shops country-fresh. Look out for a reliable supplier of organic produce, and almost everyone can grow herbs in pots on a windowsill.

Whether you want a family supper or a celebration dish, you will find just the right recipe in this superb collection. There are dishes for all occasions from substantial and nourishing soups to mouth-watering desserts and from melt-in-the-mouth pies to magnificent roasts. Wherever you live, let a breath of country-fresh air blow through your kitchen.

Home-made Stocks

A sauce or stew is only as good as the stock that it is made from. Stock is easy to make: it basically cooks itself after the first few minutes.

Fish Stock

Makes 2 litres/3⅓ pints/8 cups

INGREDIENTS
900 g/2 lb heads and bones and trimmings
    from white fish
1 onion, thinly sliced
1 carrot, thinly sliced
1 leek, thinly sliced
1 lemon, thinly sliced
8 parsley stems
1 bay leaf
250 ml/8 fl oz/1 cup dry white wine
5 ml/1 tsp black peppercorns

1 Put all the ingredients in a saucepan or flameproof casserole and cover with 1.75 litres/3 pints/7½ cups water. Bring to the boil over a medium heat, skimming off any surface foam.

2 Simmer gently for 25 minutes, then strain through a muslin-lined sieve. Cool, then chill. Reduce, if you wish, for storage or freezing.

Vegetable Stock

Makes 1.75 litres/3 pints/7½ cups

INGREDIENTS
1 onion, peeled
2 carrots
2 large celery sticks
small amounts of any of the following:
    leeks, celeriac, parsnip, turnip,
    cabbage, cauliflower, mushroom
30 ml/2 tbsp vegetable oil
1 bouquet garni
6 black peppercorns

1 Slice the onion and roughly chop the remaining vegetables. Heat the oil and fry the vegetables until soft and lightly browned. Add the remaining ingredients. Cover with 1.75 litres/ 3 pints/7½ cups water.

2 Bring to the boil, skim, then partially cover and simmer for 1½ hours. Strain and allow to cool. Store in the fridge for up to 3 days.

Beef Stock

Makes 3 litres/5 pints/12 cups

INGREDIENTS
3.6–4.5 kg/8–10 lb raw or cooked beef or
    veal bones and meat
2 large unpeeled onions, halved and
    root end trimmed
2 medium carrots, cut in large pieces
1 large celery stick, cut in
    large pieces
2 leeks, cut in large pieces
1 or 2 parsnips, cut in large pieces
2–4 garlic cloves, peeled
1 large bouquet garni
15 ml/1 tbsp black peppercorns

1 Place the bones, meat and vegetables in a large roasting tin and brown in the oven at 230°C/450°F/Gas 8 for 30–40 minutes, turning occasionally.

2 Transfer to a stock pot, add the remaining ingredients and cover with cold water by at least 2.5 cm/1 in. Bring to the boil over a medium heat. Skim off the foam with a spoon as soon as it appears, continuing until it stops.

3 Reduce the heat and simmer very gently, uncovered, for 4–5 hours. Skim occasionally and do not boil. Top up with boiling water if the level falls below the bones and vegetables.

4 Discard the bones and vegetables. Cool and chill the stock, then scrape off the fat. Remove any further fat by "wiping" with kitchen paper.

Chicken Stock

Makes 2 litres/3⅓ pints/8 cups

INGREDIENTS
2 kg/4½ lb raw chicken carcasses, necks or
    feet or cooked carcasses
2 large onions, unpeeled, root end trimmed
3 carrots, cut in large pieces
1 celery stick, cut in large pieces
1 leek, cut in large pieces
2 garlic cloves, unpeeled and lightly smashed
1 sprig fresh parsley
2 bay leaves

1 Proceed as for Beef Stock, starting at step 2, but simmer for 2 hours.

COOK'S TIP: Make stock whenever you roast a piece of meat on the bone or a bird, or save bones and carcasses in the freezer until you have enough for stock. After making stock, reduce it by at least half and freeze in an ice cube tray. Store the cubes in a freezer bag and add to soups and sauces while frozen. Never add salt to the stock as it will be concentrated during reduction and season sauces after adding the stock.

Techniques

Chopping Onions

Many dishes use chopped onions as an essential flavouring, and for stir-fried dishes it is important to keep the pieces even.

1 Peel the onion. Cut it in half and set it cut side down on a board. Make lengthways vertical cuts along it, cutting almost but not quite through to the root.

2 Make two horizontal cuts from the stalk end towards the root, but not through it. Cut the onion crossways to form small, even dice.

Chopping Vegetables

For coarsely chopped vegetables, follow the steps without shaving off curved sides. Alternatively, coarsely chop vegetables in a food processor by pulsing, but take care not to turn them into a purée.

1 Peel the vegetable, if instructed. Cut long vegetables across into pieces about 7.5 cm/3 in. Shave off curved sides.

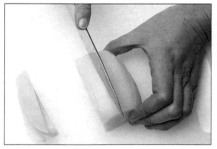

2 Lay the vegetable flat and cut it lengthways into uniform slices, according to the size required, guiding the side of the knife with your knuckles. Stack the slices and cut lengthways into uniform strips. Gather the strips together and cut across the strips into cubes or fine dice.

Blanching & Refreshing

Vegetables are blanched for several reasons: to loosen skins before peeling, to set colour and flavour, and to reduce bitterness. They are often blanched as an initial cooking, when further cooking is to be done by stir-frying or a brief reheating in butter or if they are to be used in a salad. After blanching, most foods are "refreshed" to stop them cooking any further.

1 To blanch: Immerse the food in a large pan of boiling water. Bring the water back to the boil and boil for the time specified, usually 1–2 minutes. Immediately lift the food out of the water or strain.

2 To refresh: Quickly immerse the food in iced water or hold under cold running water. If the recipe specifies, leave until it has cooled completely. Drain well.

Chopping Herbs

Chop herbs just before you use them: the flavour will then be at its best.

1 Place the leaves on a clean, dry board. Use a large, sharp cook's knife (if you use a blunt knife you will bruise the herbs rather than slice them) and chop them until they are as coarse or as fine as needed.

2 Alternatively, use a herb chopper, also called a *mezzaluna,* which is a very useful tool for finely chopping herbs or vegetables and consists of a sharp, curved blade with two handles. Use the *mezzaluna* in a see-saw motion for best results.

Celery Soup

Mild celery with a hint of nutmeg – this fresh-tasting and nourishing creamy soup makes a perfect starter.

Serves 4

INGREDIENTS
1 small head of celery
1 onion, finely chopped
1 small garlic clove, crushed
few parsley sprigs, chopped
2 bay leaves
1 thyme sprig
600 ml/1 pint/2½ cups milk
25 g/1 oz/2 tbsp butter, softened
25 g/1 oz/¼ cup plain flour
pinch of grated nutmeg
1 egg yolk, beaten
salt and freshly ground black pepper
chopped fresh parsley, to garnish
croûtons, to serve

1 Break the head of celery into stalks and wash thoroughly. Trim the root ends. Chop the stalks and leaves and put them into a large saucepan.

2 Add the onion, garlic, herbs and just enough water to cover. Bring to the boil and simmer, uncovered, over a low heat for about 35 minutes.

3 Bring the milk to the boil. Knead the butter and flour together to make a paste and whisk into the hot milk until just thickened. Cook over a low heat, stirring occasionally, for about 10 minutes. Pour into the celery mixture and cook for 5 minutes.

4 Remove and discard the bay leaves and thyme. Using a ladle, spoon the soup into a blender or food processor and process for 1 minute, until smooth. Alternatively, rub through a strainer with the back of a spoon. Return to a clean saucepan and season well.

5 Stir in the grated nutmeg and the beaten egg yolk. Bring the soup almost to boiling point, then serve garnished with chopped fresh parsley and croûtons.

COOK'S TIP: To make croûtons, cut the crusts off two thick slices of day-old bread and cut the bread into 5 mm/¼ in squares. Heat 30 ml/ 2 tbsp vegetable oil or 50 g/2 oz/ 4 tbsp butter in a frying pan and sauté the cubes, tossing and stirring constantly. Drain on kitchen paper.

Mushroom & Parsley Soup

Thickened with bread, this rich mushroom soup will warm you up on cold autumn days. It makes a terrific hearty lunch.

Serves 8

INGREDIENTS
75 g/3 oz/6 tbsp unsalted butter
900 g/2 lb field mushrooms, sliced
2 onions, roughly chopped
600 ml/1 pint/2½ cups milk
8 slices white bread
60 ml/4 tbsp chopped fresh parsley
300 ml/½ pint/1¼ cups double cream
salt and freshly ground black pepper
parsley, to garnish

2 Tear the bread into pieces, drop them into the soup and leave the bread to soak for 15 minutes.

1 Melt the butter and sauté the mushrooms and onions for about 10 minutes, until soft but not coloured. Add the milk.

3 Purée the soup and return it to the pan. Add the parsley, cream and seasoning. Re-heat, but do not allow the soup to boil. Serve with parsley.

Pumpkin Soup

A classic symbol of harvest time, pumpkin makes a beautifully coloured soup which would be perfect for an autumn dinner.

Serves 4

INGREDIENTS
50 g/2 oz/¼ cup butter
1 medium onion, finely chopped
450 g/1 lb piece of peeled pumpkin,
    cut into 2.5 cm/1 in cubes
750 ml/1¼ pints/3 cups Chicken Stock
    or water
475 ml/16 fl oz/2 cups milk
pinch of grated nutmeg, plus extra,
    for serving
40 g/1½ oz spaghetti, broken
    into small pieces
90 ml/6 tbsp freshly grated
    Parmesan cheese
salt and freshly ground black pepper

1 Heat the butter in a pan. Add the onion and cook gently for 8 minutes, until softened. Stir in the pumpkin, and cook for 3 minutes.

2 Add the stock or water and cook for about 15 minutes, until the pumpkin is tender. Remove from the heat.

3 Process the soup in a blender or food processor. Return it to the pan. Stir in the milk and nutmeg and season with salt and pepper. Bring the soup back to the boil. Stir in the spaghetti and cook until tender. Stir in the Parmesan. Serve in individual bowls sprinkled with a little nutmeg.

Baby Carrot & Fennel Soup

Sweet tender carrots find their moment of glory in this delicately spiced soup. The fennel provides a distinctive aniseed flavour without overpowering the carrots.

Serves 4

INGREDIENTS
50 g/2 oz/4 tbsp butter
1 small bunch of spring
   onions, chopped
150 g/5 oz fennel bulb, chopped
1 celery stick, chopped
450 g/1 lb new carrots, grated
2.5 ml/½ tsp ground cumin
150 g/5 oz new potatoes, diced
1.2 litres/2 pints/5 cups Chicken or
   Vegetable Stock
60 ml/4 tbsp double cream
salt and freshly ground
   black pepper
60 ml/4 tbsp chopped fresh parsley,
   to garnish

COOK'S TIP: For extra convenience, you can freeze the blended soup in portions before adding the double cream, seasoning and parsley. When you are ready to serve, defrost thoroughly and reheat the soup gently before adding the remaining ingredients.

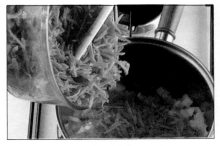

1 Melt the butter in a large saucepan and add the spring onions, fennel, celery, grated carrots and ground cumin. Cover and cook for 5 minutes, until the vegetables have softened.

2 Add the potatoes and chicken or vegetable stock, and simmer for a further 10 minutes, until the vegetables are tender.

3 Blend the mixture in the pan with a hand–held blender. Stir in the double cream and season to taste with salt and freshly ground black pepper. Serve in individual bowls and garnish with chopped fresh parsley.

Leek & Thyme Soup

A filling, heart-warming soup which can be blended to a smooth purée or served as it is here, in its original peasant style.

Serves 4

INGREDIENTS
900 g/2 lb leeks
450 g/1 lb potatoes
115 g/4 oz/½ cup butter
1 large fresh thyme sprig
300 ml/½ pint/1¼ cups milk
salt and freshly ground
   black pepper
fresh thyme,
   to garnish (optional)
60 ml/4 tbsp double cream,
   to serve

3 Melt the butter in a large saucepan and add the leeks and thyme sprig. Cover and cook for 4–5 minutes, until softened. Add the potato pieces and just enough cold water to cover the vegetables. Re-cover and cook over a low heat for 30 minutes.

4 Pour in the milk and season to taste, cover and simmer for a further 30 minutes. Some potato will break up, leaving a rather lumpy soup.

1 Top and tail the leeks. If you are using big winter leeks strip away all the coarser outer leaves, then cut the leeks into thick slices. Wash under cold running water.

2 Cut the potatoes into rough dice, about 2.5 cm/1 in, and dry thoroughly on absorbent kitchen paper.

5 Remove the thyme sprig (the leaves will have fallen into the soup) and serve, adding a tablespoon of cream and a garnish of thyme, if using.

a & Ham Soup

Once designed to satisfy the appetite after a hard day on the farm, this hearty soup is just as good after a walk in the fresh air.

Serves 4

INGREDIENTS
450 g/1 lb/2½ cups green
    split peas
4 rindless streaky
    bacon rashers
1 onion, roughly chopped
2 carrots, sliced
1 celery stick, sliced
2.4 litres/4 pints/10 cups
    cold water
1 fresh thyme sprig
2 bay leaves
1 large potato, roughly diced
1 ham hock
freshly ground black pepper

1 Put the peas into a bowl, add just enough cold water to cover and set aside to soak overnight.

2 Cut the bacon into small pieces. In a large saucepan, dry fry the bacon for 4–5 minutes, or until crisp. Remove from the pan with a slotted spoon.

VARIATION: Yellow split peas can be used instead of green, or try using a mixture of both.

3 Add the onion, carrots and celery to the fat in the pan and cook for 3–4 minutes, until the onion is softened, but not brown. Return the bacon to the pan with the water.

4 Drain the peas and add to the pan with the herbs, potato and ham hock. Bring to the boil, reduce the heat, cover and cook gently for 1 hour.

5 Remove the thyme, bay leaves and hock. Process the soup in a blender or food processor until smooth. Return to a clean pan. Cut the meat from the hock and add to the soup. Season with black pepper and serve.

Cod with Parsley Sauce

A simple, traditional dish which combines the delicate flavour of cod with a smooth herb-infused sauce.

Serves 4

INGREDIENTS
25 g/1 oz/2 tbsp butter, plus extra
    for greasing
4 cod fillets or steaks,
    about 225 g/8 oz each
1 bay leaf
6 peppercorns
small bunch of parsley
1 shallot, quartered
25 g/1 oz/¼ cup plain flour
300 ml/½ pint/1¼ cups milk
salt and freshly ground
    black pepper
cabbage, to serve (optional)

1 Grease a large flameproof casserole with a little butter. Lay the cod fillets in the pan, skin side down. Add the bay leaf, peppercorns, parsley stalks and the quartered shallot.

COOK'S TIP: For a stronger parsley flavour, try using the flat-leaved variety for this dish. If that is not available, however, the more familiar curly-leaved variety also makes an excellent sauce.

2 Pour over enough cold water to cover the fish. Bring to the boil and immediately reduce to a gentle simmer. Cook for 5 minutes. Meanwhile, finely chop the parsley tops and set aside.

3 Melt the butter in a saucepan, then stir in the flour and cook gently for 1 minute. Strain the stock from the fish and reserve 150 ml/¼ pint/⅔ cup. Remove the fish from the pan and keep warm.

4 Gradually add the reserved stock to the flour mixture and continue stirring over a medium heat until the sauce is smooth and has thickened.

5 Gradually add the milk and bring to the boil. Reduce the heat and cook the sauce, stirring occasionally, for about 10 minutes. Stir in the chopped parsley and season well. Serve with the fish and cabbage, if liked.

Mackerel with Roasted Blueberries

Fresh blueberries burst with flavour when roasted, and their sharpness complements the rich flesh of mackerel very well.

Serves 4

INGREDIENTS
15 g/½ oz/2 tbsp plain flour
4 small cooked, smoked mackerel fillets
50 g/2 oz/4 tbsp unsalted butter
juice of ½ lemon
salt and freshly ground black pepper
lettuce, orange segments and rind, to serve

FOR THE ROASTED BLUEBERRIES
450 g/1 lb blueberries
25 g/1 oz/2 tbsp caster sugar
15 g/½ oz/1 tbsp unsalted butter
salt and freshly ground black pepper

1 Preheat the oven to 200°C/400°F/ Gas 6. Season the flour. Dip each fish fillet into the flour to coat it well.

2 Dice the butter, dot it on the fish fillets and bake in the oven for 20 minutes.

3 Place the blueberries, sugar, butter and seasoning in a separate small roasting tin and roast them, basting them occasionally, for 15 minutes. Drizzle the lemon juice over the mackerel and serve with the roasted blueberries, lettuce and orange.

Griddled Trout with Bacon

If you can find it, use wild brown trout for its superb flavour, which is vastly superior to that of farmed rainbow trout.

Serves 4

INGREDIENTS
4 trout, cleaned and gutted
25 g/1 oz/¹/₄ cup plain flour
75 g/3 oz streaky bacon
50 g/2 oz/4 tbsp butter
15 ml/1 tbsp olive oil
juice of ½ lemon
salt and freshly ground
    black pepper
fresh thyme, to garnish
griddled tomatoes, to serve

2 Roll the trout in the seasoned flour mixture and wrap them tightly in the streaky bacon, apart from the heads.

3 Fry the trout in the butter and oil for 5 minutes on each side. Drizzle with lemon juice and serve with the tomatoes and garnished with thyme.

1 Pat the trout dry with absorbent paper and mix the flour and salt and pepper together.

Cod & Spinach Parcels

The best way to serve this dish is to slice each parcel into about four and reveal the large meaty flakes of white fish.

Serves 4

INGREDIENTS
4 x 175 g/6 oz pieces of thick
   cod fillet, skinned
225 g/8 oz large spinach leaves
2.5 ml/½ tsp freshly grated nutmeg
45 ml/3 tbsp white wine
salt and freshly ground black pepper
lemon wedges and chopped fresh parsley,
   to garnish

2 Blanch the spinach leaves in boiling water for a minute and refresh under cold water.

3 Pat the spinach leaves thoroughly on plenty of absorbent kitchen paper.

1 Preheat the oven to 180°C/350°F/ Gas 4. Season the fish well with salt and freshly ground black pepper.

COOK'S TIP: For best results, cover the roasting tin with a loose-fitting lid or a sheet of aluminium foil before poaching in the oven.

4 Wrap the spinach around each fish fillet. Sprinkle with nutmeg. Place in a roasting tin, pour over the wine and poach for 15 minutes. Slice and serve hot with the cooking juices drizzled over the top, garnished with the lemon wedges and parsley.

Creamy Fish & Mushroom Pie

Fish pie is a healthy and hearty dish for a hungry family. To help the fish go further, mushrooms provide both flavour and texture.

Serves 4

INGREDIENTS
butter, for greasing
225 g/8 oz assorted wild and cultivated
    mushrooms, trimmed and quartered
675 g/1½ lb cod or haddock fillet,
    skinned and diced
600 ml/1 pint/2½ cups milk, boiling
salt and freshly ground black pepper

FOR THE TOPPING
900 g/2 lb floury potatoes, quartered
25 g/1 oz/2 tbsp butter
150 ml/¼ pint/⅔ cup milk
freshly grated nutmeg

FOR THE SAUCE
50 g/2 oz/4 tbsp unsalted butter
1 medium onion, chopped
½ celery stick, chopped
50 g/2 oz/½ cup plain flour
10 ml/2 tsp lemon juice
45 ml/3 tbsp chopped fresh parsley

1 Preheat the oven to 200°C/400°F/ Gas 6. Butter an ovenproof dish, scatter the mushrooms in the base, add the fish and season with salt and pepper. Pour on the boiling milk, cover and cook in the oven for 20 minutes. Using a slotted spoon, transfer the fish and mushrooms to a 1.5 litre/2½ pint/ 6¼ cup ovenproof dish. Pour the liquid into a jug and set aside.

2 Cover the potatoes with cold water, bring to the boil, add a pinch of salt and cook for 20 minutes. Drain and mash with the butter and milk. Season well with salt, pepper and nutmeg.

3 To make the sauce, melt the butter in a saucepan, add the onion and celery and fry until soft, but not coloured. Stir in the flour, then remove from the heat.

4 Slowly add the reserved liquid, stirring well to combine. Return to the heat, stir and simmer to thicken. Add the lemon juice and parsley, season, then add to the dish.

5 Top the pie filling with the mashed potato and return to the oven for 30–40 minutes, until the topping is golden brown.

COOK'S TIP: This dish freezes well but should be completely defrosted before reheating.

27

Chicken Casserole with Blackberries & Lemon Balm

This delicious casserole combines some wonderful flavours, and the combination of red wine and blackberries gives it a dramatic appearance.

Serves 4

INGREDIENTS
4 chicken breasts, partly boned
25 g/1 oz/2 tbsp butter
15 ml/1 tbsp sunflower oil
25 g/1 oz/¼ cup flour
150 ml/¼ pint/⅔ cup red wine
150 ml/¼ pint/⅔ cup
  Chicken Stock
grated rind of ½ orange plus
  15 ml/1 tbsp juice
3 lemon balm sprigs, finely chopped,
  plus 1 sprig to garnish
150 ml/¼ pint/⅔ cup double cream
1 egg yolk
115 g/4 oz/⅔ cup fresh blackberries,
  plus 50 g/2 oz/⅓ cup to garnish
salt and freshly ground black pepper

1 Remove any skin from the chicken, and season the meat. Heat the butter with the oil in a pan, fry the chicken to seal it, then transfer to a casserole.

2 Stir the flour into the pan, then add the red wine and the chicken stock and bring to the boil, stirring. Add the orange rind and juice and the chopped lemon balm. Pour the mixture over the chicken in the casserole.

3 Preheat the oven to 180°C/350°F/Gas 4. Cover the casserole and cook in the oven for about 40 minutes.

4 Blend the cream with the egg yolk, add some of the liquid from the casserole and stir back into the dish with the blackberries (reserving those for the garnish).

5 Cover the casserole and cook for another 10–15 minutes. Serve immediately, garnished with the rest of the blackberries and a sprig of lemon balm.

cken, Leek & Parsley Pie

Crumbly pastry with a creamy chicken filling makes a substantial and tasty supper for a cold winter's evening.

Serves 4–6

INGREDIENTS
275 g/10 oz/2½ cups plain flour
pinch of salt
200 g/7 oz/scant 1 cup butter, diced
2 egg yolks

FOR THE FILLING
3 part-boned chicken breasts
flavouring ingredients (bouquet garni,
    black peppercorns, onion and carrot)
50 g/2 oz/4 tbsp butter
2 leeks, thinly sliced
50 g/2 oz/½ cup grated Cheddar cheese
25 g/1 oz/⅓ cup finely grated
    Parmesan cheese
45 ml/3 tbsp chopped fresh parsley
30 ml/2 tbsp wholegrain mustard
300 ml/½ pint/1¼ cups double cream
5 ml/1 tsp cornflour
salt and freshly ground black pepper
beaten egg, to glaze
mixed green salad, to serve

1 To make the pastry, sift the flour and salt. Blend together the butter and egg yolks in a food processor until creamy. Add the flour and process until the mixture is just coming together. Add 15 ml/1 tbsp cold water and process for a few seconds. Turn out on to a lightly floured surface and knead lightly. Wrap in clear film and chill for about 1 hour.

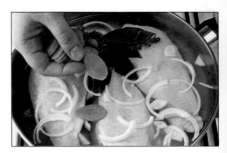

2 Meanwhile, poach the chicken breasts in water to cover, with the flavouring ingredients for about 30 minutes, until tender. Leave to cool in the liquid.

3 Preheat the oven to 200°C/400°F/ Gas 6. Divide the pastry into two pieces. Roll out the larger piece on a lightly floured surface and use to line an 18 x 28 cm/7 x 11 in pie dish. Prick the base with a fork and bake for 15 minutes. Leave to cool.

4 Lift the chicken from the poaching liquid and discard the skin and bones. Cut the flesh into strips, then set aside.

5 Gently fry the leeks in the butter over a low heat, stirring occasionally, until they are soft.

6 Stir in the cheeses and parsley. Spread half the leek mixture over the cooked pastry base, leaving a border all the way round. Cover the leek mixture with the chicken strips, then top with the remaining leek mixture.

7 Mix together the mustard, cream and cornflour in a small bowl. Add seasoning to taste. Pour over the filling.

8 Moisten the edges of the cooked pastry base. Roll out the remaining piece of pastry and use to cover the pie. Brush with beaten egg and bake for 30–40 minutes until golden. Serve hot with a mixed green salad.

31

Roast Wild Duck with Juniper

There is little meat on the leg, so one duck will serve only two people – keep the legs for making a tasty stock.

Serves 2

INGREDIENTS
15 ml/1 tbsp juniper berries, fresh if possible
1 oven-ready wild duck
   (preferably a mallard)
25 g/1 oz/2 tbsp butter, softened
45 ml/3 tbsp gin
120 ml/4 fl oz/½ cup Chicken Stock
120 ml/4 fl oz/½ cup whipping cream
salt and freshly ground black pepper
watercress, to garnish

1 Preheat the oven to 230°C/450°F/ Gas 8. Reserve a few juniper berries for garnishing and put the remainder in a heavy plastic bag. Crush coarsely with a rolling pin.

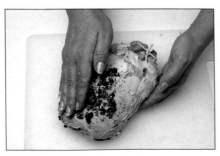

2 Wipe the duck with damp kitchen paper and remove any excess fat or skin. Tie the legs with string, then spread the butter over the duck. Sprinkle with salt and pepper and press the crushed juniper berries on to the skin.

3 Place the duck in a roasting tin and roast for 20–25 minutes, basting occasionally; the juices should run slightly pink when the thigh is pierced with a knife. Pour the juices from the cavity into the roasting tin and transfer the duck to a carving board. Cover loosely with foil and leave to stand for 10–15 minutes.

4 Skim off as much fat as possible from the roasting tin, leaving as much of the juniper as possible, and place the tin over a medium heat. Add the gin and stir to combine, scraping the base of the tin, and bring to the boil.

5 Cook until the liquid has almost evaporated, then add the stock and boil to reduce by half. Add the cream and boil for 2 minutes more, or until the sauce thickens slightly. Strain into a small saucepan and keep warm.

6 Carve the legs from the duck and reserve for stock. Separate the thigh from the drumstick. Remove the breasts and arrange the duck in a warmed dish. Pour a little sauce over, sprinkle with the reserved juniper berries and garnish with watercress.

COOK'S TIP: Use the duck carcass as well as the legs to make a duck stock for other game dishes.

Pheasant Breast with Apples

The tartness of apples perfectly complements the richness of pheasant in this wonderful traditional dish.

Serves 2

INGREDIENTS
2 boneless pheasant breasts
25 g/1 oz/2 tbsp butter
1 onion, thinly sliced
1 eating apple, peeled and quartered
10 ml/2 tsp sugar
60 ml/4 tbsp Calvados
60 ml/4 tbsp Chicken Stock
1.5 ml/¼ tsp dried thyme
1.5 ml/¼ tsp white pepper
120 ml/4 fl oz/½ cup
    whipping cream
salt
sautéed potatoes, to serve

1 With a sharp knife, score the thick end of each pheasant breast.

2 In a heavy-based frying pan melt half the butter over a medium heat. Add the onion and cook, stirring occasionally, for 8–10 minutes, until golden. Using a slotted spoon, transfer the onion to a plate.

3 Cut each apple quarter crossways into thin slices. Melt half the remaining butter in the pan and add the apple slices. Sprinkle with the sugar and cook the apple slices over a low heat, turning occasionally, for 5–7 minutes, until they are golden and caramelized. Transfer to the plate with the onion, then wipe out the pan.

4 Add the remaining butter to the pan and increase the heat to medium. Add the pheasant breasts, skin side down, and cook for 3–4 minutes, until they are golden. Turn over and cook for a further 1–2 minutes, until the juices run slightly pink when the thickest part of the meat is pierced with a knife. Transfer to a board and cover to keep warm.

COOK'S TIP: If you can't find Calvados, substitute Cognac, cider or apple juice instead.

5 Add the Calvados to the pan and boil over a high heat until reduced by half. Add the stock, thyme, a little salt and the pepper and reduce by half again. Stir in the cream, bring to the boil and cook for 1 minute. Add the sautéed onion and apple slices to the pan and cook for 1 minute.

6 Slice each pheasant breast diagonally and arrange on warmed plates. Spoon over a little sauce with the onion and apples. Serve with the sautéed potatoes.

Lamb Stew with Vegetables

Spring lamb and new vegetables make a mouth-watering combination.

Serves 6

INGREDIENTS
60 ml/4 tbsp vegetable oil
1.3 kg/3 lb lamb shoulder or other
    stewing meat, well trimmed,
    cut into 5 cm/2 in pieces
45–60 ml/3–4 tbsp plain flour
1 litre/1¾ pints/4 cups Beef or Chicken Stock
1 large bouquet garni
3 garlic cloves, lightly crushed
3 ripe tomatoes, peeled, seeded and chopped
5 ml/1 tsp tomato purée
675 g/1½ lb small potatoes, peeled if wished
12 baby carrots, trimmed and scrubbed
115 g/4 oz French beans, cut into
    5 cm/2 in pieces
25 g/1 oz/2 tbsp butter
12–18 baby onions, peeled
6 medium turnips, peeled and quartered
30 ml/2 tbsp sugar
1.5 ml/¼ tsp dried thyme
175 g/6 oz/1½ cups peas
50 g/2 oz mangetouts
45 ml/3 tbsp chopped fresh parsley
    or coriander
salt and freshly ground black pepper

1 Heat 30 ml/2 tbsp of the oil in a frying pan over a medium heat. Fry the lamb in batches, turning and adding more oil if needed. Transfer to a flameproof casserole when well browned. Add 45–60 ml/3–4 tbsp water and boil for 1 minute, scraping the base. Pour the liquid into the casserole.

2 Sprinkle the flour over the meat and set over a medium heat. Cook for 3–5 minutes until browned. Stir in the stock, bouquet garni, garlic, tomatoes, tomato purée and seasoning.

3 Bring to the boil over a high heat, skimming off any foam. Reduce the heat and simmer, stirring occasionally, for about 1 hour, until the meat is tender. Cool the stew, then chill, covered, overnight.

4 Remove all the fat from the surface. Set the casserole over a medium heat and bring to a simmer.

5 Cook the potatoes in salted water for 15–20 minutes, until tender, then using a slotted spoon, transfer to a bowl and add the carrots to the same water. Cook for 4–5 minutes, until just tender and transfer to the bowl. Add the green beans and boil for 2–3 minutes until tender. Transfer to the bowl.

6 Melt the butter in a frying pan over a medium heat. Add the onions and turnips with 45–60 ml/3–4 tbsp water and cook, covered, for 4–5 minutes. Uncover, stir in the sugar and thyme and cook, stirring occasionally, until the vegetables are caramelized. Transfer them to the bowl.

7 Add 30–45 ml/2–3 tbsp water to the pan and boil for 1 minute, scraping the base. Add to the lamb.

8 When the lamb and gravy are hot, add the vegetables and stir gently to distribute. Stir in the peas and mangetouts and cook for 5 minutes until they turn a bright green, then stir in 30 ml/2 tbsp of the parsley or coriander and pour into a warmed serving dish. Scatter over the remaining parsley.

Lamb & Leeks with Mint

This is especially good with the new season's lamb and organic leeks.

Serves 6

INGREDIENTS

30 ml/2 tbsp sunflower oil
2 kg/4½ lb lamb (fillet or boned leg), cubed
10 spring onions, thickly sliced
3 leeks, thickly sliced
15 ml/1 tbsp flour
150 ml/¼ pint/⅔ cup white wine
300 ml/½ pint/1¼ cups Chicken Stock
15 ml/1 tbsp tomato purée
15 ml/1 tbsp sugar
30 ml/2 tbsp finely chopped fresh
    mint, plus a few more leaves,
    to garnish
115 g/4 oz/1 cup dried pears, chopped
1 kg/2¼ lb potatoes, peeled and sliced
25 g/1 oz/2 tbsp melted butter
salt and freshly ground black pepper

1 Heat the oil and fry the lamb to seal it. Transfer to a casserole. Preheat the oven to 180°C/350°F/Gas 4.

2 Fry the spring onions and leeks for 1 minute, stir in the flour and cook for 1 further minute. Add the wine and stock and bring to the boil. Add the tomato purée, sugar, salt and pepper with the mint and pears and pour into the casserole. Stir, then arrange the sliced potatoes on top and brush with the melted butter.

3 Cover and bake for 1½ hours. Then increase the temperature to 200°C/400°F/Gas 6 and cook for a further 30 minutes, uncovered, to brown. Garnish with mint leaves.

Smoked Bacon & Bean Stew

Serves 6

INGREDIENTS

150 g/5 oz/¾ cup each dried black-eyed,
  pinto and cannellini beans, soaked
  overnight in cold water and drained
15 ml/1 tbsp olive oil
6 rindless smoked streaky bacon rashers
6 large country pork sausages
3 large carrots, halved
3 large onions, halved
1 small garlic bulb, separated into cloves
4 bay leaves
2 fresh thyme sprigs, plus extra to garnish
15–30 ml/1–2 tbsp dried
  green peppercorns
300 ml/½ pint/1¼ cups unsalted Vegetable
  Stock or water
300 ml/½ pint/1¼ cups red wine
salt and freshly ground black pepper

1 Boil a saucepan of water. Add the beans and boil vigorously for 30 minutes. Drain and set aside.

2 Pour the oil into a large, flameproof casserole, then lay the bacon on top. Add the sausages, carrots and onions. Peel the garlic cloves, then press them into the mixture with the herbs and peppercorns. Spoon the beans over the top.

3 Pour in the stock or water and wine. Cover and bring to the boil. Reduce the heat and cook the stew for 4–6 hours, stirring periodically and topping up the liquid if necessary.

4 Stir the mixture and season to taste. Serve garnished with thyme.

Pork with Sage, Marjoram & Celery Leaves

Pork is an inexpensive choice which is equally suitable for a family dinner or a celebration meal. The fruity purée makes a delicious change from plain apple sauce.

Serves 8

INGREDIENTS
2.75 kg/6 lb joint of pork
45 ml/3 tbsp fresh sage
15 ml/1 tbsp fresh marjoram
45 ml/3 tbsp chopped celery leaves
50 ml/2 fl oz/¼ cup cider
salt and freshly ground black pepper

FOR THE PURÉE
2 eating apples
2 bananas
15 g/½ oz/1 tbsp butter
15 ml/1 tbsp Calvados

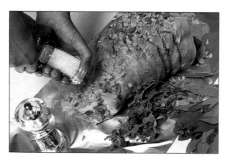

1 Preheat the oven to 160°C/325°F/ Gas 3. Place the pork in the centre of a large piece of foil. Mix the sage, marjoram and celery leaves together. Cover the fatty part of the pork with the herbs, season to taste and wrap tightly. Roast for about 1 hour.

2 Fold back the foil and baste the joint with the cider. Continue cooking, uncovered, for another hour until a sharp knife pressed into the thickest part produces clear juices.

3 To make the purée, peel and slice the apples and bananas, put the butter in a pan and sauté the fruit.

4 Add the Calvados and set it alight. When the flames have died down, remove the mixture from the heat, put it in a food processor and purée. Serve the pork with the purée on the side.

COOK'S TIP: Suitable pork cuts for roasting include loin, leg, hand and spring, and blade.

-roast Beef with Beer

This heart-warming pot-roast is ideal for a winter's supper. Brisket has the best flavour, but this dish also works well with rolled silverside or topside.

Serves 6

INGREDIENTS
30 ml/2 tbsp oil
900 g/2 lb rolled brisket of beef
275 g/10 oz onions, roughly chopped
6 celery sticks, thickly sliced
450 g/1 lb carrots, cut into large chunks
675 g/1½ lb potatoes, cut into large chunks
30 ml/2 tbsp plain flour
475 ml/16 fl oz/2 cups Beef Stock
300 ml/½ pint/1¼ cups stout
1 bay leaf
45 ml/3 tbsp chopped fresh thyme, plus
    extra, to garnish
5 ml/1 tsp brown sugar
30 ml/2 tbsp wholegrain mustard
15 ml/1 tbsp tomato purée
salt and freshly ground black pepper

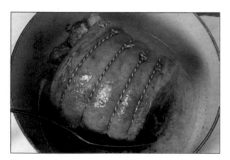

1 Preheat the oven to 180°C/350°F/ Gas 4. Heat the oil in a large flameproof casserole and brown the meat all over until it is golden. Remove from the pan and drain on kitchen paper.

2 Add the onions and cook, stirring constantly, for 4 minutes, or until beginning to soften and turn brown.

3 Add the vegetables and cook over a medium heat for 2–3 minutes, or until they are beginning to colour.

4 Add the flour and cook for a further 1 minute. Blend in the stock and stout until combined. Bring to the boil, stirring.

5 Stir in the bay leaf, thyme, sugar, mustard, tomato purée and plenty of seasoning. Place the meat on top, cover tightly and transfer to the oven.

6 Cook for about 2½ hours, or until the vegetables and meat are tender. Adjust the seasoning and add another pinch of sugar, if necessary. Sprinkle with thyme leaves. To serve, remove the meat and carve into thick slices. Serve with the vegetables and plenty of beer gravy.

ak & Kidney Pie, with Mustard & Bay Gravy

This is a sharpened-up, bay-flavoured version of a traditional favourite. The fragrant mustard, bay and parsley perfectly complement the rich, hearty flavour of the beef.

Serves 4

INGREDIENTS
450 g/1 lb puff pastry
20 g/¾ oz/3 tbsp flour
675 g/1½ lb rump steak, cubed
175 g/6 oz pig's or lamb's kidneys
25 g/1 oz/2 tbsp butter
1 medium onion, chopped
15 ml/1 tbsp made
   English mustard
2 bay leaves
15 ml/1 tbsp chopped parsley
150 ml/¼ pint/⅔ cup Beef Stock
1 egg, beaten
salt and freshly ground
   black pepper

2 Put the flour, salt and pepper in a bowl and toss the steak in the mixture. Trim and thickly slice the kidneys. Add to the steak and toss well. Melt the butter and fry the onion until soft, then add the mustard, herbs and stock and stir well.

3 Preheat the oven to 190°C/375°F/ Gas 5. Place the steak and kidney in the pie and add the stock mixture. Roll out the remaining pastry to a thickness of 3 mm/⅛ in.

1 Roll out two-thirds of the pastry on a floured surface to about 3 mm/ ⅛ in thick. Line a 1.5 litre/2½ pint/ 6¼ cup pie dish. Place a pie funnel in the middle.

4 Brush the edges of the pastry forming the lower half of the pie with beaten egg and cover with the second piece of pastry. Press together to seal, then trim. Use the trimmings to decorate the top in a leaf pattern. Brush with beaten egg and make a small hole for the funnel. Bake for about 1 hour, until golden brown.

etable Hot-pot with Cheese Triangles

Use a selection of your favourite vegetables for this wholesome dish.

Serves 6

INGREDIENTS
30 ml/2 tbsp oil
2 garlic cloves, crushed
1 onion, roughly chopped
5 ml/1 tsp mild chilli powder
450 g/1 lb potatoes, roughly chopped
450 g/1 lb celeriac, roughly chopped
350 g/12 oz carrots, roughly chopped
350 g/12 oz leeks, roughly chopped
225 g/8 oz/3 cups mushrooms, halved
20 ml/4 tsp plain flour
600 ml/1 pint/2½ cups Vegetable Stock
400 g/14 oz can chopped tomatoes
15 ml/1 tbsp tomato purée
30 ml/2 tbsp chopped fresh thyme
400 g/14 oz can kidney beans,
    drained and rinsed
salt and freshly ground black pepper
fresh thyme sprigs, to garnish (optional)

FOR THE TOPPING
115 g/4 oz/½ cup butter
225 g/8 oz/2 cups self-raising flour
115 g/4 oz/1 cup grated Cheddar cheese
30 ml/2 tbsp snipped fresh chives
about 75 ml/5 tbsp milk

1 Preheat the oven to 180°C/350°F/ Gas 4. Heat the oil in a large flameproof casserole and fry the garlic and onion for 5 minutes. Stir in the chilli powder and cook for 1 minute.

2 Add the potatoes, celeriac, carrots, leeks and mushrooms. Cook for 3–4 minutes. Stir in the flour and cook for 1 further minute.

3 Gradually stir in the stock with the tomatoes, tomato purée, thyme and seasoning. Bring to the boil, stirring. Cover and cook in the oven for 30 minutes.

4 Meanwhile, make the topping. Rub the butter into the flour, stir in half the cheese with the chives and seasoning. Add just enough milk to bind the mixture to a smooth dough.

5 Roll out the dough until it is about 2.5 cm/1 in thick and cut into 12 triangles. Brush with a little milk.

COOK'S TIP: If you do use different vegetables, remember that you may need to adjust the cooking time according to their firmness.

6 Remove the casserole from the oven, add the beans and stir to combine. Place the triangles on top, overlapping slightly, and sprinkle with the remaining cheese. Return to the oven, uncovered, for 20–25 minutes, or until golden brown and cooked through. Serve, garnished with fresh thyme sprigs, if using.

Broccoli Crumble

Quick and easy to make, melt-in-the-mouth creamy cheese-flavoured broccoli is topped with a crisp crumble.

Serves 4

INGREDIENTS
25 g/1 oz/2 tbsp butter or margarine
2 leeks, thinly sliced
25 g/1 oz/¼ cup plain flour
150 ml/¼ pint/⅔ cup milk
120 ml/4 fl oz/½ cup water
225 g/8 oz broccoli, broken
   into florets
25 g/1 oz/⅓ cup grated
   Parmesan cheese
salt and freshly ground black pepper

FOR THE TOPPING
115 g/4 oz/1 cup plain flour
5 ml/1 tsp dried basil
75 g/3 oz/6 tbsp butter or margarine
50 g/2 oz/1 cup fresh brown or
   white breadcrumbs
pinch of salt

1 Preheat the oven to 190°C/375°F/ Gas 5. Melt the butter or margarine in a flameproof casserole or saucepan and fry the sliced leeks for 2–3 minutes until they are softened.

VARIATION: You might like to try using other vegetables in this tasty dish. Cauliflower makes a good substitute for the broccoli.

2 Stir in the flour and then gradually add the milk and water. Bring to the boil, add the broccoli and simmer, half-covered, over a low heat for 5 minutes.

3 Stir in the Parmesan cheese, season with salt and pepper and pour into a medium-size ovenproof dish.

4 To make the topping, mix the flour with the basil and salt. Rub in the butter or margarine and then stir in the breadcrumbs. Sprinkle over the broccoli and bake in the oven for 20–25 minutes, until the topping is golden brown.

Leek & Onion Tart

This unusual recipe isn't a normal tart with pastry, but an all-in-one savoury slice that has a rich flavour.

Serves 4

INGREDIENTS
50 g/2 oz/4 tbsp unsalted butter
350 g/12 oz leeks, thinly sliced
225 g/8 oz onion, chopped
225 g/8 oz/2 cups
   self-raising flour
115 g/4 oz/½ cup grated hard
   white fat
150 ml/¼ pint/⅔ cup water
salt and freshly ground
   black pepper

1 Preheat the oven to 200°C/400°F/ Gas 6. Melt the butter in a heavy-based pan and sauté the leeks and onions until soft. Season to taste.

2 Off the heat add the flour, fat and water to the leek mixture in the pan. Mix well to combine.

3 Place in a greased shallow ovenproof dish that can be taken to the table and bake for 30 minutes, or until brown and crispy on the surface. Serve immediately in slices.

Creamy Layered Potatoes

Flavoured with onion and baked in a rich, creamy sauce, these would make a delicious change from roast potatoes.

Serves 6

INGREDIENTS
1.5 kg/3–3½ lb large potatoes, sliced
2 large onions, sliced
75 g/3 oz/6 tbsp unsalted butter
300 ml/½ pint/1¼ cups double cream
salt and freshly ground black pepper

1 Preheat the oven to 200°C/400°F/ Gas 6. Blanch the sliced potatoes for 2 minutes, and drain well. Place the potatoes, onions, butter and cream in a large pan, stir well and cook for about 15 minutes.

2 Transfer the potato and onion mixture to an attractive ovenproof dish. Season to taste with salt and freshly ground black pepper.

3 Bake for 1 hour, until the potatoes are tender, when pierced with the tip of a sharp knife, and lightly browned around the edges. Serve straight from the dish.

Glazed Carrots with Cider

This recipe is extremely simple to make. The carrots are cooked in the minimum of liquid to bring out the best of their flavour, and the cider adds a pleasant sharpness.

Serves 4

INGREDIENTS
450 g/1 lb young carrots
25 g/1 oz/2 tbsp butter
15 ml/1 tbsp brown sugar
120 ml/4 fl oz/½ cup cider
60 ml/4 tbsp Vegetable Stock
  or water
5 ml/1 tsp Dijon mustard
15 ml/1 tbsp finely chopped
  fresh parsley

2 Melt the butter in a frying pan, add the carrots and sauté for 4–5 minutes, stirring frequently. Sprinkle over the sugar and cook, stirring, for 1 minute, or until the sugar has melted.

3 Add the cider and stock or water, bring to the boil and stir in the Dijon mustard. Partially cover the pan and simmer for about 10–12 minutes, until the carrots are just tender. Remove the lid and continue cooking until the liquid has reduced to a thick sauce.

1 Trim the tops and bottoms of the carrots. Peel or scrape them. Using a sharp knife, cut them carefully into julienne strips.

VARIATION: For a change, try using finely chopped fresh rosemary instead of the parsley. This is an especially suitable variation for serving with roast lamb.

4 Remove the pan from the heat, and spoon into a warmed serving dish. Sprinkle the parsley over the carrots. Serve as an accompaniment to grilled meat or fish or with a vegetarian dish.

COOK'S TIP: If the carrots are cooked before the liquid in the pan has reduced, transfer them to a serving dish and rapidly boil the liquid until thick. Pour over the carrots and sprinkle with parsley.

Country Strawberry Fool

Make this delicious fool on the day you want to eat it, and chill it well, for the best strawberry taste.

Serves 4

INGREDIENTS

300 ml/½ pint/1¼ cups milk
2 egg yolks
90 g/3½ oz/scant ½ cup
    caster sugar
few drops of vanilla essence
900 g/2 lb ripe strawberries, plus 4 small
    strawberries, to decorate
juice of ½ lemon
300 ml/½ pint/1¼ cups
    double cream
4 sprigs of strawberry leaves or 4 fresh
    mint sprigs, to decorate

3 Gently heat and whisk until the mixture thickens (it should be thick enough to coat the back of a spoon). Lay a wet piece of greaseproof paper on top of the custard in the pan and leave it to cool.

1 First make the custard by whisking 30 ml/2 tbsp milk with the egg yolks, 15 ml/1 tbsp caster sugar and the vanilla essence.

2 Heat the remaining milk until it is just below boiling point. Stir the milk into the egg mixture. Rinse the pan out and return the mixture to it.

4 Purée the strawberries in a food processor or blender with the lemon juice and the remaining sugar until very smooth.

5 Lightly whip the cream and fold in the fruit purée and custard. Pour into glass dishes and decorate with the whole strawberries and strawberry leaves or mint sprigs.

h Currant Bread & Butter Pudding

Fresh mixed currants add a tart touch to this scrumptious hot pudding.

Serves 6

INGREDIENTS
8 medium-thick slices day-old bread,
   crusts removed
50 g/2 oz/¼ cup butter, softened,
   plus extra for greasing
115 g/4 oz/1 cup redcurrants
115 g/4 oz/1 cup blackcurrants
4 eggs, beaten
75 g/3 oz/6 tbsp caster sugar
475 ml/16 fl oz/2 cups creamy milk
5 ml/1 tsp pure vanilla essence
freshly grated nutmeg
30 ml/2 tbsp demerara sugar
single cream, to serve

1 Preheat the oven to 160°C/325°F/ Gas 3. Generously butter a 1.2 litre/ 2 pint/5 cup oval ovenproof dish.

2 Butter the bread generously, then halve diagonally. Layer in the dish, buttered side up, scattering the currants between the layers.

3 Beat the eggs and caster sugar lightly together in a large mixing bowl, then gradually whisk in the milk, vanilla essence and a large pinch of freshly grated nutmeg.

4 Pour the milk mixture over the bread, pushing the slices down. Scatter the demerara sugar and a little nutmeg over the top. Place the dish in a roasting tin and fill with hot water to come halfway up the sides of the dish.

5 Bake for 40 minutes, then increase the temperature to 180°C/350°F/ Gas 4 and bake for 20–25 minutes more, or until the top is golden. Cool slightly, then serve with single cream.

VARIATION: This pudding is equally delicious made with other fresh fruits. A mixture of blueberries and raspberries would work just as well.

Spiced Apple Crumble

In this version of an ever-popular dessert, hazelnuts and cardamom seeds add a spicy crunchiness to the golden topping.

Serves 4–6

INGREDIENTS
butter, for greasing
450 g/1 lb cooking apples
115 g/4 oz/1 cup blackberries
grated rind and juice of 1 orange
50 g/2 oz/¹/₄ cup light muscovado sugar
custard, to serve

FOR THE TOPPING
175 g/6 oz/1½ cups plain flour
75 g/3 oz/⅓ cup butter
75 g/3 oz/⅓ cup caster sugar
25 g/1 oz/¼ cup chopped hazelnuts
2.5 ml/½ tsp crushed cardamom seeds

1 Preheat the oven to 200°C/400°F/ Gas 6. Generously butter a 1.2 litre/ 2 pint/5 cup ovenproof dish. Peel and core the apples, then slice into the prepared dish. Level the surface, then scatter the blackberries over. Sprinkle the orange rind over the top. Mix the orange juice and muscovado sugar and then pour over the fruit.

2 Set the fruit mixture aside while you make the topping. Sift the flour into a large bowl and rub in the butter until the mixture resembles coarse breadcrumbs.

3 Stir in the caster sugar, hazelnuts and cardamom seeds. Scatter the topping over the top of the fruit.

4 Press the topping around the edges of the dish to seal in the juices. Bake for 30–35 minutes, or until the crumble is golden brown. Serve hot, with custard.

VARIATION: This crumble can be made with other types of fruit, as preferred. Rhubarb with banana, pears, gooseberries and apricots would all be delicious.

Pear & Blueberry Pie

This delicious, colourful pie, packed with autumn fruits and topped with crisp pastry, is totally irresistible.

Serves 4

INGREDIENTS
225 g/8 oz/2 cups plain flour
pinch of salt
50 g/2 oz/4 tbsp lard or vegetable
   shortening, cubed
50 g/2 oz/4 tbsp butter, cubed
675 g/1½ lb/6 cups blueberries
30 ml/2 tbsp caster sugar
15 ml/1 tbsp arrowroot
2 ripe, but firm pears, peeled,
   cored and sliced
2.5 ml/½ tsp ground cinnamon
grated rind of ½ lemon
beaten egg, to glaze
caster sugar,
   for sprinkling
crème fraîche, to serve

1 Sift the flour and salt into a bowl and rub in the lard or shortening and butter until the mixture resembles fine breadcrumbs. Stir in 45 ml/3 tbsp cold water and mix to a dough. Chill for 30 minutes.

2 Place 225 g/8 oz/2 cups of the blueberries in a pan with the caster sugar. Cover and cook gently for about 5 minutes until the blueberries have softened. Press the mixture through a nylon sieve.

3 Blend the arrowroot with 30 ml/2 tbsp cold water and add to the blueberry purée. Bring to the boil, stirring until thickened. Cool slightly.

4 Place a baking sheet in the oven and preheat to 190°C/375°F/Gas 5. Roll out just over half the pastry on a lightly floured surface and use to line a 20 cm/8 in shallow pie dish or plate.

5 Layer the remaining blueberries with the sliced pears over the pastry in the dish. Sprinkle with the ground cinnamon and lemon rind and pour the cooled blueberry purée on top.

6 Roll out the remaining pastry and use to cover the pie. Make a small slit in the centre. Brush with egg and sprinkle with caster sugar. Bake the pie on the hot baking sheet, for 40–45 minutes, until golden. Serve warm with crème fraîche.

Cheese Scones

These delicious scones make a good tea-time treat. They are best served fresh and still slightly warm.

Makes 12

INGREDIENTS
225 g/8 oz/2 cups plain flour
12 ml/2½ tsp baking powder
2.5 ml/½ tsp dry mustard powder
2.5 ml/½ tsp salt
50 g/2 oz/4 tbsp butter, chilled
75 g/3 oz/¾ cup grated Cheddar cheese
150 ml/¼ pint/⅔ cup milk
1 egg, beaten

1 Preheat the oven to 230°C/450°F/ Gas 8. Sift the flour, baking powder, mustard powder and salt into a mixing bowl. Add the butter and rub it into the flour mixture until the mixture resembles breadcrumbs. Stir in 50 g/ 2 oz/½ cup of the cheese.

2 Make a well in the centre and add the milk and egg. Mix gently and then turn the dough out on to a lightly floured surface. Roll it out and cut it into triangles or squares.

3 Brush lightly with milk and sprinkle with the remaining cheese. Leave to rest for 15 minutes, then bake the scones for 15 minutes, or until risen.

Dill & Potato Scones

Potato scones are quite scrumptious and should be more widely made.
Try this splendid combination and you are sure to be converted.

Makes 10

INGREDIENTS
225 g/8 oz/2 cups self-raising flour
40 g/1½ oz/3 tbsp butter, softened
pinch of salt
15 ml/1 tbsp finely chopped fresh dill
170 g/6 oz/scant 1 cup mashed potato,
   freshly made
30–45 ml/2–3 tbsp milk,
   as required

1 Preheat the oven to 230°C/450°F/
Gas 8. Sift the flour into a bowl, and
add the butter, salt and dill. Mix in the
mashed potato and enough milk to
make a soft, pliable dough.

2 Roll out the dough on a well-
floured surface until it is fairly thin.
Cut into neat rounds with a 7.5 cm/
3 in cutter.

3 Bake the scones on a greased
baking tray for 20–25 minutes, until
risen and golden.

First published in 1999 by Hermes House

Hermes House is an imprint of
Anness Publishing Limited
Hermes House
88-89 Blackfriars Road
London SE1 8HA

ISBN 1 84081 194 3

A CIP catalogue record for this book is available from the British Library

Publisher: Joanna Lorenz
Editor: Valerie Ferguson
Series Designer: Bobbie Colgate Stone
Designer: Andrew Heath
Editorial Reader: Penelope Goodare
Production Controller: Joanna King

Recipes contributed by: Carla Capalbo, Carole Clements, Matthew Drennan, Sarah Edmonds, Shirley Gill,
Christine Ingram, Maggie Mayhew, Katherine Richmond, Liz Trigg, Steven Wheeler, Elizabeth Wolf-Cohen.

Photography: William Adams-Lingwood, Karl Adamson, James Duncan, John Freeman,
Michelle Garrett, Amanda Heywood, Patrick McLeavey, Thomas Odulate.

1 3 5 7 9 10 8 6 4 2

Notes:
For all recipes, quantities are given in both metric and imperial measures and,
where appropriate, measures are also given in standard cups and spoons.
Follow one set, but not a mixture, because they are
not interchangeable.

Standard spoon and cup measures are level.

1 tsp = 5 ml   1 tbsp = 15 ml

1 cup = 250 ml/8 fl oz

Australian standard tablespoons are 20 ml.
Australian readers should use 3 tsp in place of 1 tbsp for measuring small quantities of gelatine,
cornflour, salt, etc.

Medium eggs are used unless otherwise stated.

Printed and bound in China